DAILY PRAYER CAPSULE

A Guide To Instructing Your Day

EUNICE RANSOME-KUTI

Dedication

Dedicated to every child of God who seeks His face through prayer.

Contents

Introduction

Often when people are prescribed medications based on diagnosis, the prescriptions are judiciously followed and, as a matter of fact, in accordance with exact times as directed by the medical practitioner without fail. Usually, adhering to the medical directives works. This then began to make me wonder why we, as Christians, do not take the supernatural daily capsules we have in the word of God.

Every day we are privileged to see a breaking of another day, we need to thank the Lord first and make declarations concerning the day as the Lord expects us to be in charge of the day. Do not be surprised that as the day breaks, lots of satanic programming, evil decrees and incantations are already programmed by the destroyer, Satan, who is the prince of the air as written in the book of Ephesians 2:2.

In Psalm 63:1, David declared, "Early will I seek thee." Joshua, Hannah, and Moses were all early risers, Jesus prayed early in the morning. With your mouth you will set the compass, the direction and the tenor; you will instruct the day to do anything for you and the day has no reason not to obey you because you will decree a thing and it will come to pass (Job 22:28).
I therefore challenge you to arise with faith, trust and confidence in God's word and decree and declare boldly as

you swallow and chew the word to set the tone for you for the day as you take charge of each day. Jeremiah 15:16 says "When your words came, I ate them; they were my joy and my heart's delight, for I bear your name, Lord God Almighty". (MSG Bible). What a feast! What delight I took in being yours, O God, God-of-the-Angel-Armies! Make it a daily practice to speak and decree these words at least three times a day. Make it a morning, afternoon and night capsule.

Confession

Thank you, Lord, for giving me another opportunity to see another day that you have made. According to your word, I will rejoice and be glad throughout today, because I have escaped again as a bird. I declare that today I shall receive the mercies of God for today which does not come to an end. Lord I acknowledge you as my Saviour and Lord and I join the 20 and 4 Elders in heaven and I worship you. Today I speak unto you that you will favour me. I declare that all elemental forces will join forces and cooperate with me to do me good in Jesus' Name. Today you will not swallow me. I will see you as I wake up every day and end the day. Today the blood of Jesus will prevail over me as I go out in the name of Jesus and come back in the name of Jesus.

You are the King of kings and the Lord of lords. You are the Lilly of the valley, the Rose of Sharon, the Bright and Morning star, the Beginning and the End, the one that can open and no man can shut, the El Shaddai, the Almighty God, the Ancient of days, the Creator of the universe who sits in heaven and makes the earth his footstool, the all-knowing God who cannot be compared with any one, the Holy One of Israel, the merciful God, I bow down with the 20 and 4 Elders and worship you. May You alone be all the Glory!

Monday

(3 Times A Day)

I declare according to the words of Psalm 23 that "the lord is my shepherd and I shall not want any good thing. I will lie down in green pastures and the Lord will lead me beside the still waters in Jesus name. I declare, according to Philippians 4:13 that "I can do everything through him who gives me strength." I will not conform any longer to the pattern of this world, according to Romans 12:2 but be transformed by the renewing of my mind to the perfect will of God in Jesus' Name. Every decree that the Lord has not commanded and spoken concerning me, my children my family and my household will not come to pass in Jesus' Name (Lamentations 3:37). The blood of Jesus will prevail for me as I cover myself and my household with it and no disease, pestilence and plague shall come near my dwelling in Jesus name (Exodus 12 verse 13).

Tuesday

(3 Times A Day)

This day I declare that my help is from the Lord who made heaven and earth. As I go out today the sun will not strike me by day nor the moon by night The Lord will preserve my going out and coming in, in Jesus' Name Amen. (Psalm 121). According to Isaiah 51:3, the LORD will surely comfort me and my household and will look with compassion on all my ruins; He will make my deserts like Eden, my wastelands like the garden of the LORD. Joy and gladness will be found in my thanksgiving and the sound of singing. Every Rod of the wicked shall not rest upon me today in Jesus' Name (Psalm 125:3). I will not be conformed to this world but shall be transformed by the renewal of my mind that by testing I may discern what is the good and acceptable and perfect will of God in the Name of Jesus. (Romans 12:2).

Wednesday

(3 Times A Day)

Hebrews 12:9 says that the Lord is a consuming fire. I decree that the fire of God will consume everything that the enemy has deposited into my pathway throughout today. The fire of God will consume everything that is not of God in my life in Jesus' Name. Numbers 23:23 says there will not be any divination and no evil omen against me and my household in Jesus' Name. Every plan and counsel against me, my family and my household will come to nought in the name of Jesus because God is with me (Isaiah 8 verse 10). I speak to the gates of this day, lift up your heads, O ye gates that the King of Glory may come in, through me, in Jesus' Name (Psalm 24: 7-10).

I will be like a tree planted by the river that bringeth forth his fruit in season. I will bring forth fruits at the right season which shall never dry up nor wither and I will prosper in whatsoever I put my hand to do in Jesus' Name (Psalm 1:3). Today I receive divine power to do God's will and commandments and as I do, I will remain on top and never at the bottom in Jesus' Name (Deuteronomy 28:13).

Thursday

(3 Times A Day)

I declare and decree that no weapon of darkness and wickedness that are formed and assembled against me shall prosper this very day in Jesus' Name. I cancel every negative and evil tongue, tongue of gossip, tongue of destruction and tongue of wickedness that rises against me in judgement. I condemn you in the anointed and mighty Name of Jesus (Isaiah 54:17). O Lord have mercy on me today for in You I take refuge. I will take refuge in the shadow of your wings until every disaster and destruction of today is passed in Jesus' Name (Psalm 57:1). O Lord I give you thanks today because you are good and your love endures forever. (1 Chronicles 16:34).

I declare that I shall abide in you and your words today and daily in Jesus' Name (John 15:7).

Friday

(3 Times A Day)

As I step out today and give my best through my skills, gifts and talents, men shall give me good measure, pressed down, shaken together, and running over in the Name of Jesus (Luke 6:38).

By the divine creative ability and deposit in me, I will manifest the gifts and the skills in me as creation is waiting for me to reveal it today in Jesus' Name. (Romans 8:19). I declare today you will supply all of my needs according to your riches in Glory. I rest in Your ability to provide for me today. I will not worry, nor complain. I declare and refuse that I will not be stressed by any lack that I see. I am aware that all my needs are completely taken care of by you in Jesus name (Philippians 4:19).

My soul bless the Lord today for all his benefits. Bless the Lord, O my soul, and all that is within me; bless his holy name! Bless the Lord, O my soul, and forget not all his benefits. The Lord forgives all my iniquity, the Lord heals all my diseases, redeems my life from the pit, crowns me with steadfast love and mercy, the Lord satisfies me with good so that my youth is renewed like the eagle's. (Psalm 103:1-5).

Saturday

(3 Times A Day)

Father I thank you because your word says that my family and I shall flourish in every department of our lives. I declare and decree that I shall flourish in my finances, my health, my relationships, my work, my career, my academic, and my spiritual life in Jesus name. My children shall make godly friends, excel in school, their education and be in good health and prosper, even as their souls prosper. (Psalm 115:14).

I will enter into your gates with thanksgiving and your courts with praise; I give you thanks for all you have done, the things you did and the things you will do and I give you praise. (Psalm 100:4).

The mark of the Lord is upon me; therefore, I declare that no man shall trouble me in Jesus name. I receive Power from above to do the will of God in Jesus' Name (1 John 2: 17). I declare and receive divine wisdom I need today and every day of my life in Jesus' Name. (James 1:5).

Sunday

(3 Times A Day)

The word of the Lord says I will be the head and not the tail. I will seek the kingdom of God and his righteousness in Jesus' Name. (Matthew 6:33).

I therefore decree that I will not be a prey to the nations, neither will the beast of the land devour me and my household and I will not be afraid of anyone in Jesus' Name according to Ezekiel 34:28. The word of the Lord will be a lamp to my feet and a light unto my path as I journey throughout today in Jesus' Name. (Psalm 119:105).

I declare that by the Grace of God, the fruit of the spirit will be evident in my life daily and I will operate and manifest them. I will also be a channel for the fruit of the spirit to draw souls to Jesus Christ. I will manifest the love of God, I will be full of the joy of the Lord which is my strength, I will experience the peace of God which passes all human understanding, I will manifest self-control, gentleness, kindness, goodness, forbearance, and faithfulness. (Galatians 5: 22-23).

Declaration

I soak all my confessions and declarations in the blood of Jesus as I see their manifestation in Jesus name.

Prayer Request

I trust you have found this prayer capsule useful to charge you daily, attract the things you need and draw you closer to God as you make your daily confessions.

If you would like us to pray with you and agree on a topic, please contact us as follows:

Reverend Dr. Eunice Ransome-Kuti
Phone (From the UK): 07984 037 163
Phone (From Abroad): +44 7984 037 163
Email: prayer@womenprayercongress.com

Notes